FROGS

by Mary Louise Bourget

Harcourt

Orlando   Boston   Dallas   Chicago   San Diego

Visit *The Learning Site!*
www.harcourtschool.com

Tadpoles come
from frog eggs.

Do tadpoles hop?
No, they swim.

Do tadpoles eat?
Yes, they eat.

Frog eggs come
from frogs.

Do frogs sing?
No, they don't.

Do frogs eat bugs?
Yes, they eat bugs.

Do frogs eat fast?
Yes, they do!